Canada's
LAND & PEOPLE

MANITOBA

Harry Beckett

Weigl

CALGARY
www.weigl.com

Published by Weigl Educational Publishers Limited
6325 10 Street SE
Calgary, Alberta   T2H 2Z9

Website: www.weigl.com
Copyright ©2008 Weigl Educational Publishers Limited

Library and Archives Canada Cataloguing in Publication

Beckett, Harry, 1936-
     Manitoba / Harry Beckett.

(Canada's land and people)
Includes index.
ISBN 978-1-55388-353-1 (bound)
ISBN 978-1-55388-354-8 (pbk.)

     1. Manitoba--Juvenile literature. I. Title. II. Series.
FC3361.2.B435 2007   j971.27   C2007-902210-3

Printed in the United States of America
1 2 3 4 5 6 7 8 9 0 11 10 09 08 07

Every reasonable effort has been made to trace ownership and to obtain permission to reprint copyright material. The publishers would be pleased to have any errors or omissions brought to their attention so that they may be corrected in subsequent printings.

We acknowledge the financial support of the Government of Canada through the Book Publishing Industry Development Program (BPIDP) for our publishing activities.

Photograph credits: Folklorama – Canada's Cultural Celebration; Where to Look Photography: page 14; Henry Kalen: page 15 middle right; Manitoba Parks: 17 bottom; Photos by Roger Matas: page 15 middle left; Mennonite Heritage Village Museum: page 15 bottom; National Archives of Canada: 13 middle right, 13 middle left; Province of Manitoba: page 4 bottom left.

Project Coordinator
Heather C. Hudak

Design
Terry Paulhus

All of the Internet URLs given in the book were valid at the time of publication. However, due to the dynamic nature of the Internet, some addresses may have changed, or sites may have ceased to exist since publication. While the author and publisher regret any inconvenience this may cause readers, no responsibility for any such changes can be accepted by either the author or the publisher.

Contents

About Manitoba

Manitoba is Canada's sixth largest province. It covers 553,556 square kilometres of land. It is nicknamed the "Keystone Province" because it is in the centre of Canada. A keystone is a stone placed in the centre of a building's arch, to balance the weight on either side.

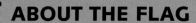

Manitoba became a province on July 15, 1870. The name *Manitoba* means "the **strait** of the Great Spirit, Manitou." The strait is Lake Manitoba. Where this lake becomes narrow, a rapping sound is made. According to Aboriginal Peoples, this is the sound of the Great Spirit Manitou beating on his drum.

A beaver wearing a crown is part of Manitoba's coat of arms. The beaver is a symbol of fur trading. The crown the beaver wears is a symbol of Manitoba's past as a British colony.

The official motto of Manitoba is *Gloriosus Et Liber*. This is Latin for "glorious and free."

ABOUT THE FLAG

Manitoba's flag was adopted in 1966. Its red background is a symbol of both Canada and Great Britain. Great Britain's flag, the Union Jack, is in the left corner. The shield of Manitoba is on the right.

LEGEND

Yukon

Northwest Territories

Nunavut

British Columbia

Alberta

Manitoba

Saskatchewan

Ontario

Quebec

Newfoundland & Labrador

Prince Edward Island

New Brunswick

Nova Scotia

N

ACTION Draw your own shield, and cut it out. Decorate it with symbols of things that are important to you. These can include your favourite people, animals, and activities.

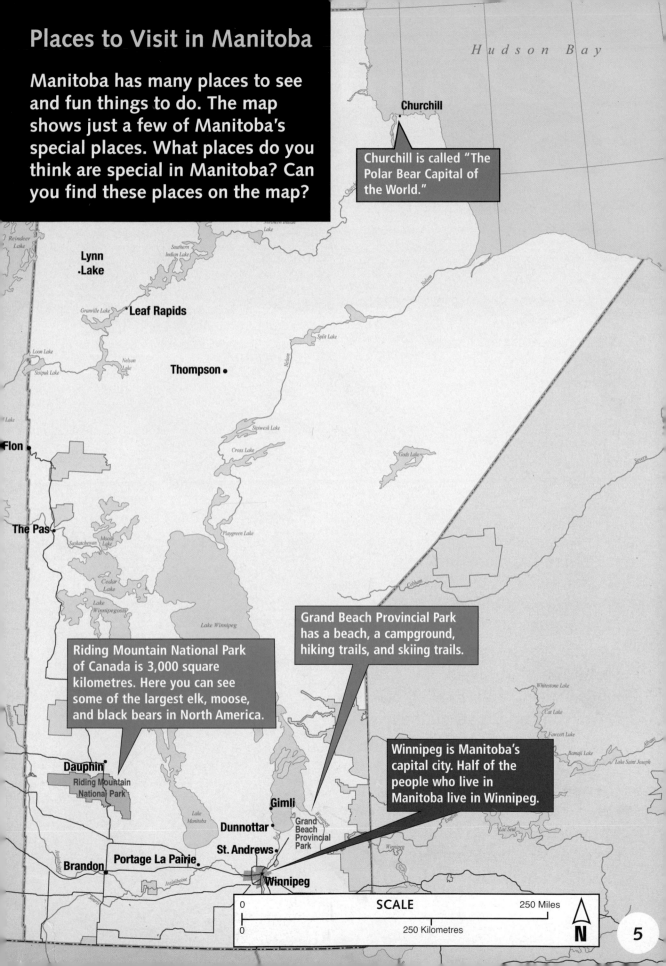

Places to Visit in Manitoba

Manitoba has many places to see and fun things to do. The map shows just a few of Manitoba's special places. What places do you think are special in Manitoba? Can you find these places on the map?

Hudson Bay

Churchill

Churchill is called "The Polar Bear Capital of the World."

Lynn Lake

Leaf Rapids

Thompson

Flon

The Pas

Grand Beach Provincial Park has a beach, a campground, hiking trails, and skiing trails.

Riding Mountain National Park of Canada is 3,000 square kilometres. Here you can see some of the largest elk, moose, and black bears in North America.

Winnipeg is Manitoba's capital city. Half of the people who live in Manitoba live in Winnipeg.

Dauphin

Riding Mountain National Park

Gimli

Dunnottar

Grand Beach Provincial Park

St. Andrews

Brandon

Portage La Prairie

Winnipeg

	SCALE	
0		250 Miles
0		250 Kilometres

N

Beautiful Landscapes

There are many different landscapes in Manitoba. These include arctic plains, sandy beaches, prairies, marshes, and forests. Prairies cover much of Manitoba. Prairies are flat, grassy lands. They are also called plains. North of Manitoba's prairies are thick forests and sparkling lakes. There are about 100,000 lakes in Manitoba. Its winters are long and cold. There is snow on the ground from November to April, sometimes October to May. Summers are short, but very warm.

The northern part of Manitoba has **coniferous forests** and watery ground, called **muskeg**. To the Far North, along the Hudson Bay, is the Hudson Bay Lowland. This is a cold, treeless area of **tundra**. The ground is covered with lichens and mosses. Caribou, mink, and wolves survive in this cold, harsh area.

Three-fifths of Manitoba is covered by the Canadian Shield. This is a large area of rocks, forests, and rivers. The Canadian Shield is 8 million square kilometres. In this area, more **Precambrian rock** can be seen than any other place on Earth.

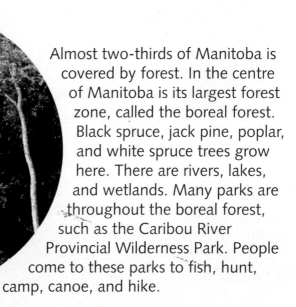

Almost two-thirds of Manitoba is covered by forest. In the centre of Manitoba is its largest forest zone, called the boreal forest. Black spruce, jack pine, poplar, and white spruce trees grow here. There are rivers, lakes, and wetlands. Many parks are throughout the boreal forest, such as the Caribou River Provincial Wilderness Park. People come to these parks to fish, hunt, camp, canoe, and hike.

Fur, Feathers, and Flowers

The bison is Manitoba's official animal. Two hundred years ago, tens of thousands of bison lived on the Manitoba prairies. They were very important to Aboriginal Peoples as a source of food. Aboriginal Peoples used the bison's dried skins to make blankets, clothing, and teepees. They used the bison's bones to make weapons and tools. Today, Manitoba is home to the third-largest bison herd in Canada, after Alberta and the Northwest Territories.

The great grey owl is the official bird of Manitoba. This owl has very good hearing, which it uses to find its **prey**. The greatest threat to the grey owl is logging. Trees are important to these owls because their nests are in trees. Young owls stay in their nests until they can fly. Great grey owls do not build their own nests. They use the empty nests of other large birds.

In 1906, schoolchildren chose the prairie crocus to be Manitoba's official flower. This flower is purple and has a furry stem. Aboriginal Peoples have used it as a medicine to treat muscle pain, nosebleeds, and cuts.

The white spruce is Manitoba's official provincial tree. This tree is found throughout the province. It is often used as a Christmas tree. Most white spruce trees live for 200 years, but they can live up to 300 years.

There are about 25,000 polar bears in the world today. Many of them live in the Far North of Manitoba. Each fall, about 1,000 polar bears walk across the frozen Hudson Bay into the town of Churchill looking for food.

Rich in Resources

Manitoba is one of Canada's three Prairie Provinces, along with Alberta and Saskatchewan. The Prairie Provinces have flat land that is good for farming. Manitoba's prairies are used to grow grains and raise ranch animals. Forests cover another large area of Manitoba. These forests provide materials for wood, paper, and other products. Manitoba also has many swift-flowing rivers. These rivers help run its **hydro-electric** plants.

One of Manitoba's most important industries is **agriculture**. Its major crop is wheat. Manitoba was Canada's first province to have a wheat industry. The province also grows barley, oats, canola, and flaxseed in its southern region.

The ancient rocks in the Canadian Shield have large amounts of **metallic ores**. The province's most important ore is nickel. Other metals mined in Manitoba are copper, zinc, and small amounts of gold and silver.

Petroleum is another natural resource in Manitoba. Petroleum is used to make fuels, such as gasoline, kerosene, diesel fuel, and jet fuel. These fuels are used to make heat and run motors.

Manitoba Hydro is the fourth-largest electrical company in Canada. It supplies hydro-electricity and natural gas to the people of Manitoba and other provinces. Manitoba's powerful rivers drive the machines that make hydro-electricity.

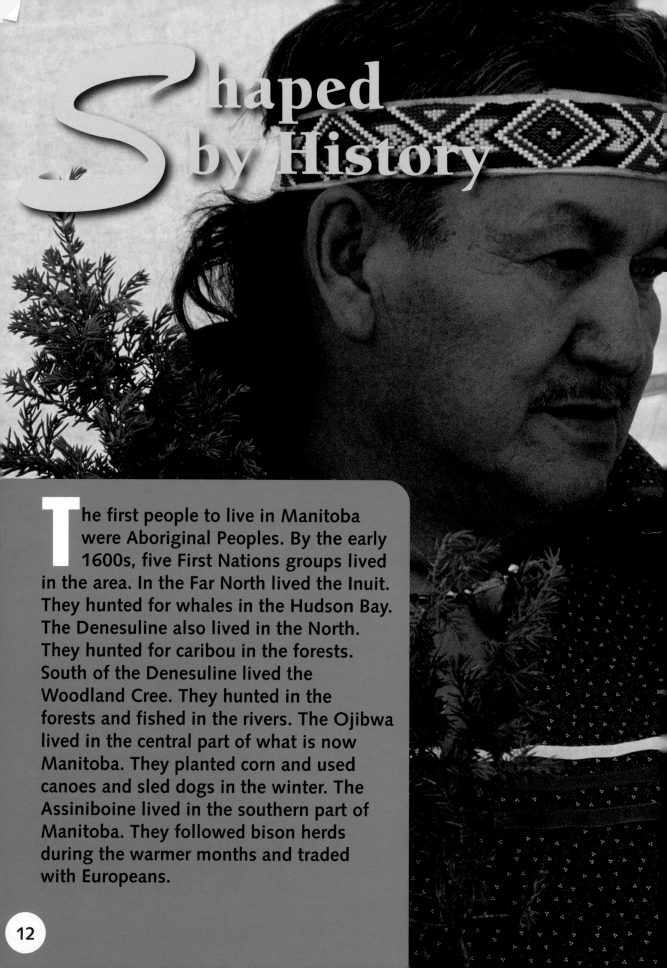

Shaped by History

The first people to live in Manitoba were Aboriginal Peoples. By the early 1600s, five First Nations groups lived in the area. In the Far North lived the Inuit. They hunted for whales in the Hudson Bay. The Denesuline also lived in the North. They hunted for caribou in the forests. South of the Denesuline lived the Woodland Cree. They hunted in the forests and fished in the rivers. The Ojibwa lived in the central part of what is now Manitoba. They planted corn and used canoes and sled dogs in the winter. The Assiniboine lived in the southern part of Manitoba. They followed bison herds during the warmer months and traded with Europeans.

Captain Thomas Button of Great Britain was the first European to reach what is now central and southern Manitoba. He claimed the area for Great Britain in 1612.

In 1611, Henry Hudson, from Great Britain, travelled to what is now called Hudson Bay. This bay is named after him. In the late 1600s, a British fur-trading company, called the Hudson's Bay Company, began business in the Hudson Bay area.

In the 1730s, France's Pierre Gaultier de Varennes and Sieur de la Vérendrye visited the Red River Valley to build trading posts. Soon, other French explorers came to this area. They also set up trading posts.

In Manitoba's early days, fur trading was the main business. However, when railroads were built in the late 1800s, the farming business began to grow. Farmers used railroads to transport grain from the fields to the markets. This system of transporting grain led to new jobs in the area. By 1881, the number of people living in Manitoba doubled.

Art and Culture

Manitoba has many cultures. To celebrate its many cultures, Manitoba holds an annual festival called Folklorama. This festival is held every August in Winnipeg. It lasts for two weeks. No other multicultural festival in the world lasts this long. During the festival, pavilions are scattered throughout Winnipeg. Each pavilion displays the culture of a certain country. These displays include food, music, dancing, and handicrafts.

The Royal Winnipeg Ballet is Canada's oldest ballet company that is still in operation. Its performers travel to other ballet centres. During these travels, they give more than 100 performances a year.

The largest heritage centre in Manitoba is the Manitoba Museum, in Winnipeg. It has eight galleries that show the history and different areas of Manitoba. The Science Gallery has a full-size **replica** of the *Nonsuch* ship. This is the ship that was sailed by British explorers in 1668 to Hudson Bay.

The Red River Exhibition is held every June to celebrate the history of Winnipeg. This event begins with a fireworks display. There are fairground rides, stage acts, children's entertainers, exhibits, and youth talent shows. The event lasts for 10 days.

The Mennonite Heritage Village is a 17-hectare village in Steinbach. This village shows the way the Mennonites lived in the 1500s. The Mennonites are a religious group of people. They are dedicated to nonviolence and to helping others. At the village, people can see early Mennonite homes made from sod, soil, grass, and wood. There is a Mennonite school from 1881, handcrafted items, and a windmill.

Points of Interest

Manitoba has many parks and outdoor activities. Every year, about 10,000 people visit northern Manitoba to see its arctic wildlife. They come to see the dazzling northern lights. These lights can be seen from a heated building called The Aurora Domes. Manitoba has many ancient **artifacts**, such as fossils. People can find fossils in the province's quarries. A quarry is a pit of ancient rock.

In the town of Churchill there are "tundra buggy" tours. A tundra buggy is a vehicle that is about 1.5 metres above the ground. It has a closed-in area for its riders. This area is heated and has windows. People ride in tundra buggies to see arctic wildlife up close. Arctic wildlife includes polar bears, black bears, wolves, moose, elk, otters, arctic foxes, arctic hares, caribou, and snowy owls.

In the spring and summer, beluga whales travel from the ocean to Hudson Bay. They come to enjoy the warmer bay water. This is a good time for whale watchers to see belugas up close. They can hear the sounds of the belugas by riding in a boat that has a special instrument called a **hydrophone**.

Thousands of years ago, Aboriginal Peoples marked their **sacred** places with special designs of wildlife, people, and objects. One of these sacred designs is called a petroform. Petroforms are made from rocks and boulders arranged into different shapes and patterns on the open ground. Some shapes look like animals. In Whiteshell Provincial Park, there is a petroform in the shape of a man. It tells the story of an Anishinabe man who asked for everlasting life from Waynaboozhoo. Waynaboozhoo is part spirit and part human, both good and evil. To make the man last forever, Waynaboozhoo turned him into a rock.

Sports and Activities

There are many types of sports and activities in Manitoba. The province's cold winter climate is perfect for winter sports, such as dog sled racing, hockey, and curling. Other activities in Manitoba are running, rock climbing, rowing, horseback riding, lake fishing, and playing tennis. The province has many golf courses and a professional football team. Warm weather sports include lawn bowling and ultimate Frisbee.

Winnipeg is home to the Manitoba Moose ice hockey team, which is part of the American Hockey League. This team plays at the MTS Centre. The Manitoba Moose Hockey Club has a charitable foundation that raises money for children's charities in Manitoba.

The Northern Manitoba Trappers' Festival began in 1916. It is the province's oldest winter festival. This annual event features a world championship dog sled race. During this race, each **musher** competes for cash prizes.

Winnipeg hosted the Pan American Games in 1967 and 1999. The Pan Am Games are a sports competition held every four years at different locations. The 1999 event included athletes from 42 countries. They competed in 38 sporting events, including karate, swimming, tennis, sailing, gymnastics, boxing, and archery.

Curling was brought to Canada long ago by people from Europe. Curling is a game played on ice with granite stones. The players slide the stones toward a target area, called "the house." The Manitoba Curling Association Bonspiel is one of the world's largest curling competitions. The word *bonspiel* is Scottish. It means "game" or "league."

What Others Are Saying

Many people have great things to say about Manitoba.

June 6, 1934 - Joy: "Joy came to the hearts of everyone in this district when on Monday afternoon it commenced to rain and continued throughout the afternoon and part of the evening, in all about half an inch...Farmers in this district are busily making plans to locate feed and land in northern Manitoba where they can move their stock."

"It is safe to say that no new country, not even excepting British Columbia and the Lake of the Woods gold districts, is attracting so much attention at this time as the great Dauphin district with its vast areas of undeveloped farm lands of superior quality, its stores of timber and fuel, its well-watered cattle runs and hay lands, and its known sources (mostly undeveloped) of natural wealth."

"The Red River Settlement is the home of a stable population, hardy, industrious, and thrifty; occupying a fine farming country with all the advantages of prairie and timber combined...and for hundreds of miles beyond stretches one of the most magnificent agricultural regions in the world, watered abundantly with lakes...."

"Imagine a land as rich in heritage as it is in wheat. A land where the horizon stretches on seemingly forever, where the sky is vast and blue, and where every sunset is an occasion to remember. Now discover what all such a land has to offer."

ACTION Think about the place where you live. Come up with some words to describe your province, city, or community. Are there rolling hills and deep valleys? Can you see trees or lakes? What are some of the features of the land, people, and buildings that make your home special? Use these words to write a paragraph about the place where you live.

Test Your Knowledge

What have you learned about Manitoba?
Try answering the following questions.

1 What is Manitoba's nickname? Why was it given this nickname?

2 What is the capital of Manitoba?

3 What company began in the Hudson Bay area in the late 1600s? Why do you think this company wanted to do business in North America? Research at the library or online to learn more.

4 What annual festival celebrates the many cultures of Manitoba?

Plan a Vacation

Imagine you are going to visit Manitoba. What are the top five things you would like to do there? Would you like to ride on a tundra buggy and see the polar bears? What about going to the Royal Winnipeg Ballet or touring a museum? Look at the map of Manitoba on page 4. How long will it take to travel to each of these places?

Further Research

Books

To find out more about Manitoba and other Canadian provinces and territories, visit your local library. Most libraries have computers that connect to a database for researching information. If you input a key word, you will be provided with a list of books in the library that contain information on that topic. Non-fiction books are arranged numerically, using their call number. Fiction books are organized alphabetically by the author's last name.

Websites

The World Wide Web is also a good source of information. Reliable websites usually include government sites, educational sites, and online encyclopedias. Visit the following sites to learn more about Manitoba.

Go to the Government of Manitoba's website to learn about the province's government, history, and climate.
www.gov.mb.ca

Visit "Canada for Kids" to learn more about Manitoba and take photo tours.
www.kathimitchell.com

Check out A to Z Kids Stuff Canada, at
www.atozkidsstuff.com/canada.
Scroll down to "Manitoba," and click on "Polar Bear Invasion" to learn how Canadian towns deal with the annual gathering of polar bears.

Glossary

agriculture: the business of raising crops and farm animals

artifacts: ancient objects, such as tools, weapons, and ornaments

coniferous forests: forests with trees that have cones, such as a pine cone

hydro-electric: electricity made by using the force of moving water

hydrophone: an electrical instrument that picks up underwater sounds

metallic ores: rock containing metal-bearing minerals

musher: the person who drives a dog sled; to make the dogs run, the musher calls out, "Mush"

muskeg: a low-lying area of soft waterlogged ground and standing water

Precambrian rock: the oldest rock on Earth, between 4.5 billion and 540 million years old

prey: an animal hunted or caught for food

replica: a copy that is very similar to its original

sacred: having a special, religious importance

strait: a narrow section that connects two bodies of water

tundra: a treeless, mossy, and windy plain

Index